# Read This When You Don't Need Advice

Like therapy. But cheaper and with jokes.

Aarzoo Maria

BookLeaf
Publishing
India | USA | UK

Made with ❤ on the BookLeaf Publishing Platform

www.bookleafpub.in

www.bookleafpub.com

# Dedication

*This is dedicated to all those who truly saw me — and those who didn't.*
*To the ones who kept growing, who tried to understand, support, and relate.*
*This isn't just a leap of faith to recharge my inner writer — it's a reminder to myself and my readers that we've always been More Than That.*

# Preface

**This isn't a guidebook.**

It's also not the kind of thing you read with a highlighter and a cup of coffee while "romanticizing healing."

It's more like a group chat that spirals into 2am truths. I didn't write this because I have it all figured out.

I wrote it because no one else seemed to be talking about this stuff — at least not in a way that didn't make me roll my eyes or Google "escape plan."

There's no moral-of-the-story energy here. Just stories. Thoughts. Truth bombs. Half-baked advice.

Things I wish someone had told me when I was pretending to have it together — or when I really, really didn't.

You'll meet my younger self in these pages: confused, embarrassed, dramatic (with good reason), and trying to unlearn all the crap I was taught to quietly accept.

So if you're tired of perfect Instagram captions...

If the words "self-love journey" make you want to throw a slipper...

Or if you just want to feel a little less alone in the mess

—

**Hi. You're holding the right book.**

# Acknowledgements

This book was written somewhere between overthinking, crying, trying to work, and pretending to be fine on Google Meet.

To everyone who said, "Just be confident" — no offense, but that was useless.

To my friends who read my rants, laughed at the bad jokes, and reminded me that my voice matters — thank you for holding space.

To my family, for giving me room to grow (even when they didn't always understand what I was growing into).

To my nani-ma, nana-ji, and dadi-maa, badde papa — who left too soon but are still looking after me.

To the version of me that thought she wasn't enough — thank you for being wrong.

This book is for all of you.

For the teenagers who are just starting to figure it out — confused, curious, and wondering if it ever gets easier.

For the adults who don't know how they got here, and need someone to say:

Whatever you've felt, gone through, or broken down over — it mattered.

There's a reason.

It's common to feel feelings.

And no, you're not the only one trying to quietly survive

in a loud world.

Thank you for picking this up.

I hope it feels like a hug in the middle of your mess.

Cover design by my very talented friend —
Nemika Bharaj

# 1

# "NEVER TALK BACK"

**Don't Talk Back**

Remember when you were tiny and would get into those harmless little arguments with your parents?

"Test diya ya topi pehnayi?"

"Tiffin khatam kiya ya sabzi wapas le aaye?"

"Class bunk ki thi kya?"

"Koi chakkar-vakkar toh nahi chal raha?"

Now, regardless of what your answer was — even if it was just a simple "yes" or "no" — your parents would somehow declare your clarification an argument, and hit you with the higher-pitched classic:

**"Don't talk back."**

Cut to me — working full-time, doing fine on paper, but still not the most confident person in the room. I second-guess everything I say. I explain things too much. I share too much sometimes, just to make sure I've said enough. Basically, I've become someone who *over-functions*, just to make sure I don't disappoint anyone.

Like a self-cleaning vacuum. One that identifies the issue, diagnoses the emotional blockage, and tries to fix it — while making a weird whirring noise and quietly panicking on the inside.

And I'd love to say I've fixed it all.

But I haven't.

Five years into corporate life, and it's still a massive win if I manage to say "Good morning" on a Zoom call. Or unmute myself to say "Hi, am I audible?" Or even "Thanks for the meeting."

That's peak performance.

I behave like Courage, the Cowardly Dog if my manager so much as glances at my laptop and says, "Can you share your screen?"

And presentations?

Please. I'd rather ride a deadly roller coaster blindfolded than open a deck and walk people through Q2 numbers.

So what do I do when it gets too much?

I escape. I start planning my imaginary business — the one I'll start "someday," where no one can ask me to present, or raise my hand, or speak when I'm not ready.

Have I opened that business?

No.

Will I?

Sure.

Now I know — maybe you picked up this chapter

thinking it would help you overcome that fear.

But it won't.

Because I'm not a psychologist.

I'm just a human who's tried to feel things and understand them. I don't have the answers. I'm not able to help myself all the time. But I'm trying.

And honestly, sometimes, *just trying* is enough.

And when it all gets too much? Run. Disappear for a bit. Take a break.

Sometimes that's not weakness — it's a reset. And it opens doors even you hadn't imagined.

But here's one thing I do know — from lived experience, from fumbling, from watching carefully:

The people who make it?

They're not always the smartest. They're just the ones who can *fake it* long enough to believe it themselves.

I learned this in postgrad.

I'd walk into class thinking everyone around me had it all figured out — average English, solid arguments, intimidating confidence. But after a few months, I realised they didn't actually know more than me. They just *thought* less about how they sounded. They mispronounced things. They rambled. But they kept raising their hands. They kept showing up.

And guess what? People listened.

That's when it clicked.

In most rooms, if you're talking about something even

remotely close to your job — the audience probably knows less than you.

It's like that school dance rule: No one knows the choreography. If you forget your steps, just keep dancing. Smile. Move. They'll never know.

But let me tell you what really lies beneath all this. When you grow up constantly being told *not to talk back*, what you're really learning is to **hold your thoughts back**. You start internalising that your questions aren't valid, that your voice is unimportant, or that your perspective might not make sense at all. So you stay quiet.

You don't raise your hand. You don't share the idea. Your heartbeat races faster than a Ferrari in an F1 race — and you just stay still.

But here's the sad truth:

The world doesn't wait for you to gather courage.

It reads your silence as disinterest.

It labels you as the quiet one, the underconfident one, the one who doesn't want it enough.

It's unfair. It shouldn't happen.

But it does.

And it took me 27 years to learn that if you don't speak, *someone else will.*

Most people are conditioned to push ahead. And maybe, you're not. But that doesn't mean you stay behind.

I'm still figuring out how to speak without feeling dumb.

I'm still unlearning the idea that every time I speak up, it's not an argument.

And even if it *is* — maybe that's okay.

Maybe I should learn to own it.

Turns out, *talking back* is exactly what I need to learn how to do.

Not with my parents anymore.

Now, it's with the world.

And if all else fails — take a deep breath.

In for 6 seconds.

Hold for 6.

Out for 7.

Repeat it a few times and pretend you're a monk instead of a panicking PPT operator.

It won't fix everything.

But it might remind you that you're still here. Still trying.

And that's something.

CHAPTER TWO

# "WHAT'S WITH THE FACES"

Imagine you're in school. It's a test day. You're helping a friend copy — being the loyal little Robin to their Batman — and suddenly the teacher calls you out.

Now technically, it's *they* who were cheating, not you. But you're a better friend than that. And anyway, snitching isn't going to help your case.

So you just stretch one side of your lip. Not a smile, not a smirk. Just a tiny twitch.

Boom. That's it. You're done. You made *a face*.

The teacher notices. They point it out in front of 60 children like you just threatened national security. You want to disappear.

Cut to: Your mom. She's scolding you for not finishing your milk. You want to tell her that it's curdled — and for once, it actually is — but you've used that excuse too many times before. So you stay quiet, and this time, you frown just a little. That's all it takes.

Now you've got an *attitude problem.*

Here's what no one tells you:
 Your face — your completely natural, human face — becomes this unpredictable liability.

No one calls it expression.
 It's labelled "judgmental," "disrespectful," or "over-smart."

You don't get to be expressive. You're told to be *appropriate.*

Now fast forward to adulthood.

You're in a meeting. Someone says something so wildly irrelevant, it physically hurts. And your face? Oh, it reacts. Subtly — but obviously.

Your boss, who can read you like a tabloid, turns and asks:

**"What do you think?"**

You're now caught between your real opinion, your diplomacy skills, and your face — which has already betrayed you.

If you don't match your expression with something coherent in words, you're either going to sound mean or, worse, *unprepared.* So you fumble, and now you're the problem.

Honestly, the only plus side to having an expressive face is that it makes you a great radar. You can spot a bad idea from three PowerPoint slides away.

But then comes the darker side.

You know those moments where you laugh at the wrong time? Or smile when someone shares something tragic? Or look confused when someone is crying?

It's not because you're a psychopath.

It's because your face doesn't know how to behave under pressure.

And sometimes... neither do you.

So here's my expert (non-expert) advice:

**Either hide your face behind a friend who knows you can't help it. Or turn your face completely and look at a wall.**

Conceal that doomed face like a dacoit, for all I care — but do it.

The world's just not ready for that kind of honesty yet.

But real talk?

We're taught so early to control our expressions, we start suppressing *everything*. We get so used to being told "fix your tone," "control your look," "what will people think"— that we begin to doubt our natural instincts.

You stop trusting your reactions.

You start filtering yourself before anyone even asks you to.

You start fearing that just *looking* a certain way might

get you in trouble.

And the worst part? Sometimes it does.

But if you're like me — someone who feels first and reacts faster — then let me say this clearly:
There's nothing wrong with your face.
 The problem is that too many people around you are uncomfortable with honesty.
 Even if it's written across your eyebrows.
So go on. Be expressive.
 But maybe carry a scarf. Just in case someone dies mid-conversation and your face reacts *a little too quickly*.
Baby steps.

# CHAPTER THREE

# "YOU CAN'T DO IT"

There are all kinds of people around us — especially the ones who think they know us better than we know ourselves. I wouldn't have minded that if their opinions were helpful, or even kind. But somehow, they always know what we *can't* do.

If I'm a boy, I shouldn't learn Kathak.

If I'm a girl, I shouldn't learn Taekwondo.

Because god forbid, we do something *unexpected.*

But like... what if I'm surrounded by eve-teasers one day, and my self-defence move is a full-on Kathak toda?

You'll never see it coming. *Chakkar and chakku, both ready.*

Then there are the other people — the ones who know your poop cycle, your periods, your breakdown triggers. Your real ones. The ones who remind you not to doubt yourself. Even when you're at your lowest, they look at you and go,

"Try toh kar. What's the worst that'll happen?"

These people?

Keep them close. Frame them if you can.

Now let's talk about the third kind.

If you're anything like your author (hi), you're powered by *negative motivation.*

You don't need a vision board. You need a nemesis.

You can spot these people by their aura — even when they're smiling and saying the right things, you can feel that passive red laser beam passing through your soul. They're not saying "you can't" directly, but you *know* they don't believe in you. And that's all the motivation you need.

These people?

Also keep them close. Not emotionally — just close enough to prove them wrong.

But on a serious note — you will, at some point, find yourself in that weird, tight-chested space where it's just you against the world.

You're 23+.

You're earning.

You're paying bills.

You're waking up for meetings.

Eating khichdi at 9 p.m.

And quietly fighting every single thing inside you — without making a scene.

It's not unusual. But it's not ideal either.

And in that space, you'll need something that brings you peace. A pet. A friend. A walk. A playlist. Your partner. Or God.

And no — choosing a spiritual path doesn't make you uncool. It doesn't make you weak or extra or "one of those people." It just means you've found a place where your brain can breathe a little.

Because when the whole world feels like it's against you, and you start believing that voice in your head that says, *"You really can't do this..."*

Remind yourself:

You are somebody's child.

If nothing else, you are God's child.

And that's enough of a reason to keep going.

Be an opportunist.

Life doesn't wait.

Ask for that project.

Apply for that job.

Say yes to that open mic.

DM that person you've been too shy to text.

Do the thing.

Because people are out there — waiting to grab those same things.

And even if you *think* there's no space for you, I promise — there is.

Even if your brain whispers, *"no chance"*,

I'm here to tell you:

**You do.**

And look — validation feels like sunlight. Like you're watering this dream inside you.

But wait too long for other people's claps, and it quietly becomes a trap.

The more you wait for people to say *you're ready*,

The longer you delay what you were always meant to do.

Do it anyway.

Before they even get the chance to say you can't.

# CHAPTER FOUR

# "IT'S NOT ABOUT YOU"

I once coloured Gandhi ji yellow in my kindergarten years.

You know what my teacher did?

She got the whole class to clap for me.

Bless her soul — not because Gandhi ji is actually yellow (he isn't), but because my colouring was clean, symmetrical, and *within the lines*. That was the win. Not accuracy. Not creativity. Just neatness.

We're told early on what "being good" looks like — and when we don't fit that exact image, we start feeling like maybe we're just... extra. Or invisible.

So if you've ever felt like you're *not* the main character in your own life — just because your dance teacher didn't put you in the centre, or your boss didn't give you five stars in your appraisal, or your parents won't stop comparing you to that prodigy child who won a quiz at age 3 — then this one's for you.

And before you think I'm about to tell you *"you're not average, you're different"* — don't worry, I'm not. That's not the point.

Sometimes the point is this:
 Pretend you're in a movie. Act like the lead.
 Or do something weird enough to remind yourself you *are* the story.

Let me tell you about someone I know.
 We'll call him Ajay.

Tall, dark, handsome. Married. Has a kid. He's decently okay at his job — nothing extraordinary. But you know what makes him stand out?

His absolute indifference to everything. Like, truly everything.

 You could tell him, "Ajay, Sonal fell down the stairs," and he'd go:

 **"So?"**

You ask, "Ajay, what do you love about fruits?"

 **"Fruits are fruits. Doesn't matter."**

Try to talk deep, like "Ajay, what do you think about the universe?"

 **"Everyone is mortal."**

I don't know if it's an act.
 I just know that somehow, it *works*.

Women are still attracted to his mysterious nonchalance.

It's giving *zero effort, full effect.*

Now, if you can't pull off that level of weird detachment, don't worry — most of us can't. But that leaves you with a few other options: mainly, learning to stop needing other people to see you as the hero in your story.

And look, I get it. Sometimes you just want someone to notice. To say, "Hey, that thing you did — that mattered." Even if it was small. Even if it was just showing up when you didn't want to. Sometimes we don't need applause — we just want to be seen.

But the hard truth? Most people are too busy starring in their own drama to even register your scene.

The real question is:

Do you not *feel* like the hero in your life?

Or do you just hate that other people don't *see* you that way?

Because the second one doesn't matter.

The older you grow, the more you realise:

People barely think about you. Even if you punch them in the face, they'll probably forget by the next group dinner.

So instead of waiting for centre stage or outside applause — act like it's your world and everyone else is just doing cameos.

If you want to paint a politician pink, paint him pink.
If you say the inside of a watermelon is red, then it's red.
If you believe in it — confidently, boldly, and slightly delusionally — then people might start believing in it too.
Maybe I coloured Gandhi ji yellow because I didn't know better. Or maybe I just liked how neat it looked. Maybe that's the whole point — the world doesn't always reward truth, it rewards conviction. So have some.
You don't need to be loud. Or original. Or impressive. You just need to show up like you matter — even when no one's clapping.

## CHAPTER FIVE

# "You're Too Young for This"

This is nothing but the youngest child POV on the world. The author (hi) grew up in a typical Punjabi joint family. A little *Hum Saath Saath Hain* moment, at least on the surface. Life was good.

A few days back, someone was talking about how they used to get extra test papers for their younger sibling. How they'd take them to extra classes and tutor them at home.

Couldn't relate at all.

I was on the other end of that spectrum — the one where *I* was the reason everyone had to pause their life. Wait for me to finish that glass of milk. Then puke. Then drink it again. Or the times my cousins had to cover up for my class bunks. Or my incomplete homework. Or my very dramatic excuses.

So many *had-tos*.

As the youngest duckling, I've also been kicked out of family gossips and secrets — some I still don't know about. I wasn't included in card games or cousin jokes. They seldom played with me — I was "too small" or "too delicate."

Then came the teenage years — where you finally start earning your place in the OG cousin group.

And that's when the real revelations begin. No one tells you anything. It all just gets displayed in front of you like breaking news.

I didn't know when my eldest brother had his first drink. Didn't know when another one, a lifelong vegetarian, started eating fish.

Didn't know when my sister had her first boyfriend. Not gonna lie — I used to feel bad.

Left out. Unseen. Like I wasn't in on the real stuff. But I made my own world.

Played by myself when no one was around.

And the best part? I started enjoying it. I never felt lonely when I was alone — in fact, I started craving it when I wasn't.

If I'm not wrong, I think the non-coddled youngest children turn out like this.

A few years passed, and somehow, I moved out. And suddenly, I was getting 13 calls a day from different family members — at different hours — asking everything from "khaana khaya?" to "pankha band kiya kya?"

My roommate was out of India at the time, and I remember my *chachi* asking me,

"Don't you get scared sleeping alone at night?"

And I just wanted to say — I live for this.

Alone. Peaceful. Independent.

Honestly, saying I enjoy living alone would be an understatement.

I'm addicted to it.

But in my family, I'm still that child who isn't asked for opinions.

Not involved in decisions.

No one expects me to handle anything remotely "important."

Even locking the door at night is someone else's job.

And truthfully?

I just exist.

And I'm fine with it.

Having said that — it's not always the best thing in the world.

The slightest inconvenience makes me run to someone.

And then something happened that I'll never forget.

I took my parents to Vietnam.

The first three days of the trip were wonderful.

But soon, the language gap hit hard. The locals mostly

spoke Vietnamese, and my parents couldn't manage on their own — which meant everything depended on me. I thought I was acing it.

But honestly? I was losing it. The heat, the constant coordination, the stress.

Then came Halong Bay — and things went south.

My dad started getting sick. His BP dropped.

Speech started slurring. Fever shot up.

And me — the girl who's terrified of hospitals — ran him straight into one.

Spent nights there.

Cried in the washroom.

Fought the anxiety.

My dad — being the "youngest" sibling in *his* family too — threw a full tantrum.

"I'm not spending another day in a hospital. Take me home."

So I did what I had to.

I got our flights preponed.

Scored a discount on the hospital bill.

Arranged for his BP monitor, fruit juices, emergency meds.

Called doctors back in India. Got alternate opinions.

For context: the doctors in Vietnam said he wasn't fit to fly.

But a doctor in India said, "Bring him if that's what he wants. Just be ready with a few in-flight exercises... in case."

I could hear my ears go numb.

All I wanted was to bring him home — safely.

And I didn't want him to suffer. At all.

Many cries, anxious nights, and whispered prayers later — we landed.

And I grew up that day.

Didn't even realise I had it in me.

We spend so much time thinking we're too young. Too soft. Too under-prepared.

But we've been watching.

We've been learning.

We've been collecting quiet lessons — and we use them when it matters.

Now I know — I *can* handle any situation if I really need to.

But do I want to?

**No.**

Do I still want to be babied?

**Absolutely.**

# CHAPTER SIX

# "It is What it is"

Your author is a small-town Indian girlie — in case you hadn't guessed.

And in this part of the world, you don't learn soft skills like cooking or cleaning or folding bed sheets because they're life skills. You learn them so that one day, when you're married off and sent to "the boy's house," no one questions your parents' upbringing.

You must know how to make *everything*, clean *everything*, serve *everyone* — not for yourself, but so your family name doesn't get dragged in the post-wedding gossip.

And I know this isn't the first time you're hearing this. If you're a man reading this: everything I'm about to say is just to help you walk in our age-old, inherited shoes — the ones we're still being made to wear.

 And if you're a woman — you'll probably be fuming with relatability by the end of this.

Let's rewind to the early 2000s.

My mom used to make my brother and me mop the floor. Later, when she proudly told people that her *children* did this chore, she'd always add, "My son did it so well. He's really good at it."

Not that he wasn't.

But... was I not? Or did it just not count because, well, I'm *supposed* to be good at it by default? My brother gets applause for trying. I get expectations. No extra credit for doing what's expected of you.

I kept trying. Rarely heard anything nice.

Then came the serving duty.

Mom's food is ready. All the kids are glued to *CID* or *Crime Patrol.* Guess who gets called to serve the food? "Because I said so," she'd say.

And just to keep things "equal," once in a thousand years, my brother would be asked to do it too. As a treat. A PR move.

But the limits really got tested the day we went to meet a girl's family — a match for my cousin. We were *guests.* And one of my relatives gave me the classic desi family eye signal — time to get up and serve.

Wait, what? I'm the guest here too!

But there I was — serving my family, and hers.

Oh, and I have to tell you this one also.

I was at home — my home — when a close uncle yelled from the other room:

24

"*Ae ladki, paani pila.*"

Now, this uncle has a habit of calling me "ladki" — like I'm an extra from a Bhojpuri film set. No name. No tone. Just function.

I still got him water.

Then he asked me to get some for the other uncles in the drawing room.

Then again for himself. Then again. All with zero decency or respect.

At the time, I didn't even realise how wrong it was. But my mom did.

She said, "It's not okay. If it doesn't feel okay, speak up."

Cut to now: I'm a fully independent woman.

Earn my own money. Pay my bills. Travel alone. Book tickets. Sign contracts. Get scammed and then unscammed. I do it all.

And you know who raised me?

That same mother — the one who taught me about financial independence, *and* how to fold a saree blouse like my future in-laws might inspect it.

It took me years to realise that our moms don't always do this because they want to shrink us — they do it because they're trying to protect us.

They want to prepare us for what *they* know is coming. Because most times — it does.

But here's the tricky part: when mothers grow up, they sometimes become what they once despised.

They forget the cages they broke free from — and build new ones for their daughters.

You know what they say: "What we don't heal, we hand down."

Our generation is smart — we *see* this now.

But that's not enough. It's not enough to spot the pattern.

We need to break it. Destroy it. Do *whatever* it takes to raise a generation with **zero bias** — and give them *quality* before TikTok does.

And before you think I'm done... let's talk about real tests of feminism.

You say you're all for equality. Great.

Now your brother gets married. A new girl walks into your house.

She's your sister-in-law. Your bhabhi.

And now, you have a choice.

You either treat her like you wish your in-laws would treat you someday...

Or you treat her like the *new joinee* in your family office.

Keep her out of the loop. Make her earn her place. Gossip about her "adjustments."

Make her feel like a guest in the very house she's moved into.

And if she ever opens up to you — tells you she feels isolated or overwhelmed — and your response is,

*"It is what it is"...*

Then congratulations, you've become the problem.
There's nothing wrong with running a household. My
mother does, and she's amazing at it.
 But believing that it's *all* a woman is meant to do?
Yeah, that mindset's cancelled.


Life is beautiful.
 And women — they're the reason it looks like art
sometimes.
Keep them happy, and watch how they bring colour,
light, and calm into the most chaotic rooms.
And to all the women who are fighting silent fights —
who are doing everything with a smile but planning
their freedom in the quiet of their minds —
Keep going.
 But *really plan it.*
 Because no one else is planning it for you.
They might want to protect you like a delicate bird — but
you were built to fly, not perch.
 And the world? You're supposed to see all of it.
And while you're up there — be a girl's girl.
And take your bestie along.

# CHAPTER SEVEN

# "RESPECT YOUR ELDERS"

The second you're born into an Indian household, you're not just a baby.

You're a walking debt.

Because diapers, vaccines, admission forms, and tuitions — they're all investments.

And the EMI? It's paid through one lifelong expectation: "Respect your elders."

And don't get me wrong — many elders *do* deserve it.

The ones who raised you with patience. The ones who were there at your worst.

The ones who clapped when you didn't win, and comforted you when you didn't lose either — you just... felt low.

That kind of elder? Give them your respect. Your time. Your everything.

But let's talk about the *other* kind.

The kind who pop up once every few years —
 not to ask how you are, but to ask what your salary is now.

The kind who never helped you with your maths homework but still have opinions on your marks.

The kind who will never ask if you're okay —
 but will discuss your mental health with 14 other relatives *because they're "worried".*

You know the ones.

 They'll never check in.

 But they'll check your outfit.

 And if you're with a boy? Oh ho. Alert the news channels.

They'll correct your behaviour in public, talk about your insecurities in front of guests, and still expect you to touch their feet after it.

And if you say anything back?

"Tameez naam ki cheez nahi hai!"

Here's a truth bomb I wish someone had handed me earlier:

Respect isn't a one-size-fits-all rule.

 Just because someone is older doesn't mean they're right.

 And it definitely doesn't mean they've earned your space, your story, or your respect.

This?

This is what we're unlearning.
This is what no one ever told us —
Not in school,
Not in moral science class,
Not even in those long, useless "values" assemblies
where they made you recite things no one believed.
Age is not a pass.
It's not a license to comment, control, or casually hurt.
Now, I'm not saying go out there and disrespect
everyone over 50.
What I *am* saying is — choose your elders.
Not everyone with grey hair and an opinion is your
mentor.
If they've never shown up for you — emotionally,
mentally, even with a little kindness —
you don't owe them more than a nod and a civil smile.
So no, I won't fetch water for that uncle who doesn't
remember my name.
And no, I won't explain my life decisions to an aunty
who still thinks being single at 30 is a curse.
Because respect, just like love and trust, is earned.
And when you're old enough to think for yourself,
you're also old enough to say:
"Not this time, uncle."

# CHAPTER EIGHT

# "STUDY NOW PLAY LATER"

❦

This is nothing but the youngest child POV on the world. The author (hi) grew up in a typical Punjabi joint family. A little *Hum Saath Saath Hain* moment, at least on the surface. Life was good.

A few days back, someone was talking about how they used to get extra test papers for their younger sibling. How they'd take them to extra classes and tutor them at home.

Couldn't relate at all.

I was on the other end of that spectrum — the one where *I* was the reason everyone had to pause their life. Wait for me to finish that glass of milk. Then puke. Then drink it again. Or the times my cousins had to cover up for my class bunks. Or my incomplete homework. Or my very dramatic excuses.

31

So many *had-tos*.

As the youngest duckling, I've also been kicked out of family gossips and secrets — some I still don't know about. I wasn't included in card games or cousin jokes. They seldom played with me — I was "too small" or "too delicate."

Then came the teenage years — where you finally start earning your place in the OG cousin group.

And that's when the real revelations begin. No one tells you anything. It all just gets displayed in front of you like breaking news.

I didn't know when my eldest brother had his first drink. Didn't know when another one, a lifelong vegetarian, started eating fish.

Didn't know when my sister had her first boyfriend. Not gonna lie — I used to feel bad.

Left out. Unseen. Like I wasn't in on the real stuff. But I made my own world.

Played by myself when no one was around.

And the best part? I started enjoying it. I never felt lonely when I was alone — in fact, I started craving it when I wasn't.

If I'm not wrong, I think the non-coddled youngest children turn out like this.

A few years passed, and somehow, I moved out. And suddenly, I was getting 13 calls a day from different family members — at different hours — asking everything from "khaana khaya?" to "pankha band kiya kya?"

My roommate was out of India at the time, and I remember my *chachi* asking me,

"Don't you get scared sleeping alone at night?"

And I just wanted to say — I live for this.

Alone. Peaceful. Independent.

Honestly, saying I enjoy living alone would be an understatement.

I'm addicted to it.

But in my family, I'm still that child who isn't asked for opinions.

Not involved in decisions.

No one expects me to handle anything remotely "important."

Even locking the door at night is someone else's job.

And truthfully?

I just exist.

And I'm fine with it.

Having said that — it's not always the best thing in the world.

The slightest inconvenience makes me run to someone.

And then something happened that I'll never forget.

I took my parents to Vietnam.

The first three days of the trip were wonderful.

But soon, the language gap hit hard. The locals mostly

spoke Vietnamese, and my parents couldn't manage on their own — which meant everything depended on me.

I thought I was acing it.

But honestly? I was losing it. The heat, the constant coordination, the stress.

Then came Halong Bay — and things went south.

My dad started getting sick. His BP dropped.

Speech started slurring. Fever shot up.

And me — the girl who's terrified of hospitals — ran him straight into one.

Spent nights there.

Cried in the washroom.

Fought the anxiety.

My dad — being the "youngest" sibling in *his* family too — threw a full tantrum.

"I'm not spending another day in a hospital. Take me home."

So I did what I had to.

I got our flights preponed.

Scored a discount on the hospital bill.

Arranged for his BP monitor, fruit juices, emergency meds.

Called doctors back in India. Got alternate opinions.

For context: the doctors in Vietnam said he wasn't fit to fly.

But a doctor in India said, "Bring him if that's what he wants. Just be ready with a few in-flight exercises... in case."

I could hear my ears go numb.

All I wanted was to bring him home — safely.

And I didn't want him to suffer. At all.

Many cries, anxious nights, and whispered prayers later — we landed.

And I grew up that day.

Didn't even realise I had it in me.

We spend so much time thinking we're too young. Too soft. Too under-prepared.

But we've been watching.

We've been learning.

We've been collecting quiet lessons — and we use them when it matters.

Now I know — I *can* handle any situation if I really need to.

But do I want to?

**No.**

Do I still want to be babied?

**Absolutely.**

## CHAPTER NINE

# "YOU CAN'T HAVE FUN 3 DAYS IN A ROW"

Best week of the year? Easy. Your best friend's birthday on Thursday. Farewell party on Friday. Date on Saturday. I remember when this miracle-of-a-week appeared in my life. My mom could sniff it from a mile away.

The minute I'd channel my full 'poo energy' to get ready, she'd start dragging out my flaws — not just from this life, but from my previous two janams minimum.

My wardrobe? Messy.

My homework? Incomplete.

My chair? Piled with clothes.

My soul? Apparently corrupted by the *idea* of too much fun.

And I was a child with too much self-respect to argue. So I'd cry, defend, cancel plans — the whole sad montage. And weirdly, that always felt like the goal. Wasn't it?

I don't blame her entirely. She was a victim too — of boredom, societal pressure, and the legendary Indian fear of too much enjoyment.

Because here's the truth: desi households treat fun like it's heroin. Addictive. Dangerous. Forbidden.

And the minute you look like you're enjoying life too much, people assume one of two things:

- You're irresponsible.
- Or you're *that* kind of kid. (You know the one — short skirt, loud laugh, probably has a boyfriend.)

But don't think being an introvert saves you either. If you stay home, they'll call you boring. Spineless. Dumb.

So here's the harsh truth: they're going to talk *either way*. And sometimes, even your parents — the people who love you most — won't be able to shut them up.

It's a painful way to grow up. Especially in a small town. But here's my advice: get your comebacks ready.

Whether it's a relative, neighbour, or a family friend with nothing better to do — hit back with charm and wit.

If your parents can afford your fun, amazing.

If they can't? Earn it yourself. Take that job, buy your own Friday outfit, and plan your own weekends. Because you weren't born to live in fear of being seen at a party.

**Life's too short to be explained to aunties and uncles.**

So yes — have fun.

Three days in a row. Six nights in a week.

Just don't forget to do it sincerely.

Not to prove anything. Not to rebel.

Just because joy — when earned and owned — is the purest resistance of all.

## CHAPTER TEN

# "You'll Miss It When We're Gone"

Before you read this — just a heads-up.

This one might get a little emotional. So if your heart's feeling soft today, you might want to come back to it later.

 Or don't. Sometimes, it's okay to feel everything at once.

You know, as kids and teens, we grow up dreaming of freedom. Of independence. Of figuring out who we *really* are — all those big, exciting, TED-Talky words.

But no one tells you that growing up also means leaving behind things you never imagined you'd miss.

I still remember something a senior said on farewell day:

**"पिंजरे में कैद थे, जब निकले तो पिंजरे से प्यार हो चुका था।"**

He wasn't just talking about school. He was talking about everything that felt like a cage — the curfews, the rules, the overprotectiveness — that suddenly turns into comfort the second you walk away from it.

You turn 18, pack up your bags, and move to a city that feels like a stranger. But soon, you start building a life. You make friends, you start calling your flatmates your second family, you get used to the tap leaking and the fridge not working and the random guy shouting "Kabadiiiii" at 2pm.

This new place? It starts feeling like home. Just like your real one.

And then comes the next phase.

You start working. You're in your 20s. You have your own money now — and **a lot less energy**. The pressure kicks in. Weekdays blur into meetings. Weekends disappear into laundry and bills. Your idea of joy isn't partying anymore — it's peace. You stop chasing excitement and start chasing naps.

And somewhere in between, something shifts.

You start missing home. And not in the "I want maa ke haath ka rajma" way.

In the "I want to sit next to her in the kitchen while she cuts bhindi" way.

In the "I want to ask Papa if he's okay, even when he says he is" way.

Suddenly, those two days at home never feel enough. You want one more night. You want to stay longer. Because now, you're noticing things you didn't before. Like how your dad breathes a little slower. Or how your mom's phone has more reminders than she used to need. They're growing older, and for the first time, you're aware of it. Painfully, constantly aware.

You start worrying: *Are they eating right? Who do they talk to when I'm not there? Do they feel lonely?*

And then, something happens that breaks you in a way nothing else has — your grandparents pass away.

And for the first time ever, you don't see your parents as just your parents.

You see them as children.

Children who just lost their parents.

And that? That feeling is indescribable.

You don't grieve for your loss. You grieve for theirs.

You want to ask them, *"Are you okay?"*

But you also know they won't really say if they're not. Because that's how they were raised — to keep going. Quietly.

And deep down, a terrifying thought creeps in: *One day, this will be me.*

And yet, we avoid it. We push it away. Because we're too scared to even think about it. Our hearts? Too soft. Too meek to handle that kind of ache.

But listen — if you're anything like me, you need to hear

this:

**Our parents are strong.**

Stronger than we give them credit for.

They miss us every second — yes.

But they also know how to adapt. How to survive the silence. How to make peace with the distance.

And no — that doesn't mean you *should* stay away.

If life lets you live close to them, please do.

But if you can't — because of work, life, the world — then don't let guilt eat you alive. That's not why they raised you.

They didn't raise you to be constantly afraid of disappointing them.

They raised you so that one day, when you were on your own, you'd know how to stand up. How to cook. How to cry. How to pay rent. How to chase dreams.

But will we ever stop needing their love, their affection, and those 36 missed calls?

**Never.**

Will we ever let them be anything other than our parents?

**Not in this lifetime.**

So I don't have a big message here. No clever closing line.

Just this:

*Spend time, money, effort, everything — on them.*

Tell them things you think they already know.

Take that surprise flight. Answer that random "Kya kar rahi ho?" call.

Because why not?

They're your home.

And no matter how far you go — they always will be.

# CHAPTER ELEVEN

# "ITS ALL IN YOUR HEAD"

You know what I miss about childhood?

Doing dumb things with pride. No guilt, no overthinking, no "I should've handled that better." Just vibes.

Cut to adulting: your body suddenly feels like it's 55, your back cracks louder than your laugh, and your sugar levels are one dessert away from "borderline." And of course, anxiety shows up like it owns the place.

Uninvited, unbothered, unavoidable.

The worst part? Nobody takes it seriously.

Say "I had anxiety last week" and watch people either trauma-dump their own story or nod like you told them you stubbed your toe. It's like being colour-blind — invisible to everyone except the one living with it.

Let me tell you what anxiety actually feels like:

It's not cute.

It's not quirky.

And no, it's not *just in your head.*

It's when your brain feels like it's overheating.

When your hands shake, your heart races (and not in the romantic way), and you forget how to breathe. You start crying without permission, and your anxiety? It starts having anxiety.

It's like your own body is hijacking you.

And you're trapped inside, just watching.

You know what's worse? No one can help. People either say,

"You think too much."

"Have ajwain water."

"Go to sleep."

If it worked like that, I'd be cured every time I blinked. Sometimes, people will just *listen.* And those are the people you hold close — not because they fixed it, but because they didn't make it worse.

I remember this one time at work — a proper corporate intervention. Someone got mad because I didn't attend an unplanned meeting. Not a client call, not a deadline — just a random meeting I wasn't looped into. Suddenly I was being called "disrespectful" in a tone that made it feel like I had punched someone's dad.

And I just sat there — trying to explain myself, watching

45

my own body betray me. The words weren't coming out. But the tears were.

I wasn't sad. I was just angry. Furious. Humiliated.

So I left the room, found another, and froze. I sobbed. I wheezed. I couldn't catch my breath. My manager tried to help. I couldn't respond. And all I could think was:

*"Do they deserve to see me like this?"*

And the scarier thought:

*"Do I deserve to feel like this?"*

That was the day I realised — this wasn't nervousness.
It had a name. Anxiety.
And I hated it.

It crept in like smoke. Quiet, invisible, but choking everything. I started dreading every conversation, every meeting, every "Can I talk to you for a minute?"

People noticed. Some took advantage. Most ignored.
That's how it works. The world doesn't wait for your healing. Especially not the corporate world — where your silence looks like weakness, and your breakdown becomes gossip by lunch.

No one's going to give you a mental health day because you're feeling anxious. Even a cold has better chances.

So what do you do?

You learn to mask it.

You learn to function with fire in your chest.

You learn to make to-do lists while your brain screams.

You learn to walk through it — because lying down never helped.

I'm not saying don't seek help. Please do.

But if you're still saving for that one therapy session, here's what you *can* do:

Walk. Not to escape — but to move through it.

Blast your music. Let your body outrun your thoughts.

Give your brain a deadline — "Okay, overthink till 8 p.m., then we move on."

Don't show it to everyone. Not because it's shameful — but because not everyone deserves to see you soft.

And if you're expecting your family to understand?

Good luck. They'll hand you fennel water and ask you to chant somethings 11 times. You'll get more sympathy for a sore throat.

Anxiety is like a stray dog on the road — it senses fear. And if you flinch, it comes closer.

So walk like you own the street. Even if your legs are shaking. Even if your breath's short.

You can cry later. First, survive the day.

And please — don't let it define you.

You are not your panic.

You are not your bad week.

You are not weak.

You're just human. And your brain? It's fighting too.

So hold your ground.

Put your poker face on.

And when in doubt — be a cow.

Yes, a cow.

Wander. Chew. Chill in the middle of the road.

The world will make space for you.

They always slow down for a cow.

# CHAPTER TWELVE

# "GET OFF YOUR PHONE"

There's this new trend I've been noticing among new parents — and I call it the *no-screen-time experiment*. You'll hear them say things like:

*"We don't show our child any videos while feeding them."*

*"No phones within 200 metres of the baby, radiation is harmful!"*

*"No Baby Shark — it's addictive!"*

Cute. Adorable, even. But give it a year. I've been silently observing. And trust me — they *always* cave.

That vow lasts about as long as a teething phase.

Within a year, the screen slips in — while they take that one emergency office call, or FaceTime nani-nana, or just need 10 minutes of peace. The phone isn't a tool anymore. It's an extra limb.

Now's parents are us. Millennials. Borderline Gen Zs.
From recipes to affirmations to catching up with the world, everything we need is on the phone.
And you don't even realise how many times you use it in front of your child —
that long-overdue catch-up call, a scroll before bed, or just checking "something quickly" and then vanishing into the void.
They're watching.
Children up to 5 imitate *everything*. Even the misdeeds.
So either you give up your phone entirely...
or you accept the inevitable: they'll get used to it.
Hold on — I'm not asking you to hand toddlers an iPad with their bottle.
But let's be real — you can't ban something from their lives when *you live on it.*
Where do you think the future is going?
They're not going to be writing on slates.
They'll be using tablets for school, YouTube for concepts, ChatGPT to finish essays, and tech in ways we can't even imagine yet.
You'll scream *"Switch off Netflix!"*
They'll smile and cast it from another device.
Because that's what we did when our parents tried to stop us.
But oh — **our childhood? That was something else.**
Evening hangouts with colony friends.

Inventing games out of pure boredom.
Making chocolate cake out of literal mud.
(*No regrets — just worms and strong immunity.*)

I remember when I was 10, and *Roadies* was a thing.
The hot guy was Ranvijay, and we were the contestants.
That was what we are playing now.
Cringe? Yes.
Unforgettable? Also yes.
One of our *self-created tasks* was to ring a stranger's
doorbell and cartwheel back without getting caught.
*High risk, zero prize, full entertainment.*

I'm not underselling Netflix. I love a good binge too.
But I'd give it up in a heartbeat if someone knocked on
my door and said, "Come play downstairs."
Even if it's stappoo (not even from my generation) or
*kho kho.*
Look — binge-watching is fun. I won't pretend I haven't
done a full weekend with snacks, Netflix, and zero
shame. But I'd give it up in a heartbeat if someone
knocked on my door and said, "Come play downstairs."
Even if it's *kho kho.*
Because here's the truth:
**Anyone can scroll.**
**But not everyone can make real memories.**
So while you're still free from EMIs, deadlines, and back

pain — play.

Be silly.

Be outside.

Be the main character in your own Roadies episode.

Because adulting isn't half as fun as you think.

And Netflix will wait.

## CHAPTER THIRTEEN

# "WHAT'S THAT TIME OF THE MONTH"

Boys and girls are the same — until they're not.

Right around the time girls start entering their *babe era*, the universe throws in a little blood and chaos, like a welcome gift from hell. It begins with pain that feels illegal, underwear that dies a heroic death, and a feeling that maybe, just maybe, you're quietly being punished for turning into a woman.

If you're lucky, someone tells you it's normal.

If you're not, they act like it's your fault.

And in some homes, they just don't tell you anything at all.

Mine was one of those.

In school, there was going to be a period seminar. The kind with a screen and cartoon diagrams and an

awkward lady talking about pads like she's giving a TED Talk. But our school, in its deep-rooted parental approval obsession, asked for consent slips signed by parents.
The next day, I showed up — the *only* girl in the *entire school* without one.

Everyone else had their parental blessing to go learn about the mysterious thing happening to their bodies. I, apparently, wasn't allowed to know. Because my parents believed that if I learned about periods... I'd start getting them. Like it was a curse you could unlock by watching an explainer video.

So there I was, confused, humiliated, and completely out of the loop. I faked a stomach ache and begged my sister to pick me up early. I didn't even fully know what periods were. I just knew I was somehow in trouble for existing in a body that was growing up.

When the other girls returned, they had this weird pride — and a free pad each, like a party favour. I remember thinking, "So this is it? This is what all the fuss is about?"
No one explained anything to me. Meanwhile, the boys sat in class wondering if we were learning how to tie better ponytails or hem our skirts.

A year later, a boy I was close to once asked, with complete sincerity,
"So... do you girls pee in your panty? Is that what Whisper is for?"

II wanted to crawl under the desk. Not because he was wrong — but because I'd been trained to think even the *question* was shameful. What even more tragic was that this was the best information he had access to. No one had taught him. He was as in the dark as I was.

We were all in this broken system, pretending that half the class didn't bleed every month, and the other half didn't need to know anything about it.

But what if they *had* been told?

What if, instead of keeping it a girls-only secret, we let boys in too? What if we taught them how the uterus works? That periods aren't just "blood" but an entire biological process involving hormones, mood changes, pain, fatigue, and real chemical shifts?

What if they knew that:

- PMS is not made-up drama, it's real — hormone-induced physical and emotional changes that affect over 90% of menstruators.
- Period blood isn't gross or toxic; it's mostly uterine tissue, not even the same as what comes out of a cut.
- Cramps can be as painful as a heart attack. That's not exaggeration — that's data.
- Some girls faint. Some vomit. Some can't stand up straight. All while smiling through a school day or a board meeting.

- Pads, tampons, and menstrual cups are not "ew" — they're basic tools. Hygiene, not horror.

Maybe if we taught that in schools, boys wouldn't snicker at a pad falling out of a bag. Maybe they'd stop saying "Are you PMS-ing?" like it's a personality flaw. Maybe they'd grow up knowing how to help — not how to hide.

And maybe, we'd all stop pretending periods are something to be whispered about behind bathroom doors.

So here's the truth no one told us clearly enough:

Periods *do* make you moody. They *do* make you tired. They *do* make you want to bite your boyfriend's head off and cry about a pigeon in the same hour. But they don't make you weak. Or dirty. Or less capable.

And knowing about them — even if you don't have them — that doesn't make you awkward.

It makes you a better human.

# CHAPTER FOURTEEN

# "FAMILY FIRST"

I have a feeling this one's going to hit home for most of you. Why? Because this plays out in every Indian household.

There are some relationships we're expected to maintain —like a subscription to society. Your immediate family. Your not-so-immediate family. Relatives. Family friends. Your own friends. And those 4 people. You *know* who I'm talking about. Never forget them.

Now, depending on your upbringing, almost every relationship—except your friends—is put on a pedestal. You have to show up. Call once every two weeks. And definitely if someone has diarrhoea or their daughter is getting married.

If they're visiting, your house must look like *no one* lives there. That clean. That pristine. Impression matters. (Please note, I'm not talking about immediate family here. But if it's your mom visiting? Oh, then the cleaning part still stays.)

Now tell me—have you *ever* felt this pressure with your *friends*? Have your parents ever forced you to go hang with them at 5 AM on a Sunday? But if it's your distant aunt's daughter who's visiting, suddenly they'll offer you money, guilt, and sometimes even an emotional TED Talk to go meet her. Like yes, let me cancel a date with someone I actually like... for this forced interaction that will most likely end in joint silence and forced smiles. And these relatives? Half the time they're not even nice to your parents. Just like your parents have a sixth sense for your toxic friends, *you* now have the same radar for problematic relatives. But still, your family keeps calling, texting, showing up—because "relationships are hard to build, easy to break."

Now flip to adult friendships. The ones you make after 21. The ones who see you when you're tired, jaded, full of rage about your manager, sobbing about your ex, and eating noodles like it's a sport. They meet the version of you *you* chose to be. Not your school topper self, not your overachieving cousin self—just you.

And if your childhood friends are still around? They've probably lost all guest privileges by now. They might even have a spare key to your house. They'll walk in, open your fridge, ask why there's no cold water, and throw themselves on your bed like it's theirs. And yet when they need you—you'll *run*. Because how can you not?

Meanwhile, your aunt's daughter probably doesn't want to meet you either. But here we are, sharing family updates and pretending this is bonding.

I've often been held hostage at home because "someone is coming to visit." I've missed birthdays, hangouts, even meet-cutes with potentially hot people. But how do you explain that? That said—sometimes, these people *do* show up. Not always out of love, but out of habit. Because we showed up once too. And weirdly, the circle continues.

So, I've learnt that even if you don't want to, sometimes it helps to engage. Talk about the weather. It's the family version of saying "hi" without opening your soul. Because someday, when you're standing in a hospital queue, Agarwal uncle might just know someone who can fast-track your admission.

Not saying your friends wouldn't do that too. But... just in case.

And listen—I know not all relatives are saints. But neither are all friends. Take it with a pinch of salt. Or a tequila shot, depending on how your week's been.

I remember in grad school, one friend had a stupid fight with another girl. I jumped in with full loyalty, even though I had *nothing* to do with it. Later, they made up inside a tent. Their two "gangs" went for dinner. I stood outside. Alone. For an hour. And then heard her bitch about me *to* that same girl. Behind my back. Inside the tent.

Yes, I'm still holding onto it. Yes, I will write a show about it one day.

All I'm trying to say is: not everyone belongs in your inner circle. But some people? They can exist in the casual layer. The outer orbit. The weather-talk zone. Maintain that. It doesn't have to be emotional. Just functional. You never know when someone from that layer might pull through.

Having said that, if you force me to hang with your cousin over my friend's birthday again... I might fake a fever. Or diarrhoea. Let's keep it full circle.

## CHAPTER FIFTEEN

# "Focus on Your Studies, Not on Relationships"

If this line doesn't hit home, I don't know what will.

If you were lucky, maybe you had your first brush with love in school. The Cadbury Silk, the folded-up notes, the hand-holding near the back gate. You thought you'd get married someday, maybe live in the hills.

And then your Indian parents found out.

The look of pure betrayal. The horrified silence. That sad shake of the head that says "we raised you better." And you're what—14? 16? Still learning how to log in to Facebook properly. You don't know whether to fight for love or break up with the "love of your life."

I had a buffer zone—my cousins. They found out first.

Not that they softened the blow. They went *straight* to my dad.

But my dad's reaction? Iconic.

When he found out, I was already asleep, heart pounding. I woke up and he was sitting beside me—he hadn't slept all night. He took me to his office the next day and hit me with full-page wisdom.

He said, *"If you hold hands with a boy, it'll come in the next day's paper. If you kiss, it'll come in the paper. Boys are deceivers. Don't waste your time."*

(He wasn't wrong about *everything*, honestly.)

I loved my dad too much to rebel, so I got my act together and became a solo Cinderella.

But not everyone gets that version of the story. For many, that discovery moment leads to being screamed at —or worse. And it leaves scars you carry quietly for years.

I don't know what's right or wrong. I know that love, especially at that age, can be distracting and sometimes destructive. But it can also be magic. It's a once-in-a-lifetime kind of thing. Like test-driving a chair before you buy it forever.

If you're in that phase right now and your parents don't get it, just hold on.

Here's a secret I've probably already told you:

Your parents grow up too.

The day they see you making your own choices with

maturity, they'll understand you're ready—for love, for life, for all of it. Because real relationships aren't just about roses and dates. They're about showing up when it's inconvenient. It's work. Hard, patient, unglamorous work.

When you're older, you won't want sparks—you'll want peace. You'll want someone to split a dosa with after a long day. Someone to sit on the couch with, talking about weather and taxes and life. That's love too. That's love especially.

There's still magic in high school love. It's messy and exciting and silly and sweet. But the real magic happens when you grow into someone who knows how to love *and* how to dream, chase goals, build something.

Because here's the thing: love isn't always 50-50. Sometimes it's 70–30. Or 90–10. And when you're ready to commit to that kind of rhythm—when you know who you are and what you want—that's when you're ready for love.

Whether it happens in high school, in your 30s, or in a supermarket queue on a Tuesday.

Just don't forget—you *will* disappoint people along the way.

And that's more than okay.

## CHAPTER SIXTEEN

# "MONEY CANT BUY HAPPINESS"

Someone once said, "Money can't buy happiness."
I don't know who they were, but I'm guessing they never had to decide between taking a cab or three autos and a heatstroke to reach work.

Let's be real — whoever said that, lied. Or had generational wealth.

They tell you these things to keep you grounded.
hey say it to keep you grounded. But while they're preaching detachment, they'll happily lend ₹10 Lakhs to a cousin they secretly resent.

Nobody actually *teaches* you how important money is. They just wrap it up in moral science quotes and move on.

But here's the truth no one spells out:

That aesthetic life you romanticise on Instagram? It's

64

not funded by good vibes.

It's paid for by someone's parents — or someone's overtime. Someone's exhaustion.

I remember seeing my friends fly off to London and Australia during summer break, while we... didn't.

We didn't have the money — or the intent.

Still, I romanticised their lives. The casual tripping, the airport selfies, the oversized headphones.

Now that I earn enough to travel twice a year, I sometimes forget to be grateful.

It's wild how fast privilege stops feeling like privilege once it becomes familiar.

I saw this quote once, mid-rant about not getting enough credit at work:

*What a privilege — to be overwhelmed by the life you once dreamed of.*

Felt like a personal attack. But a necessary one.

My dad always says, "You don't need a lot of money to live a good life."

And honestly, I've felt that.

You don't need to be filthy rich — that's a choice, not a necessity.

But to live a happy, healthy, *comfortable* life?

You need *just enough* to fight inflation. To say yes to good things without guilt.

Now don't get me wrong — I'm a strong believer in money.

Not in a greedy way. But in a grounding, motivating way.

Because the absence of it? Swallows up *every* other dream.

There were two moments when money really hit different for me.

First — when I could buy something without asking my parents. A solo trip. A nice dinner. A dress I didn't overthink. Just... because I could.

Second — when I started doing yearly donation drives on Father's Day.

Feeding people. Watching those small smiles. My heart felt full.

That money felt *meaningless* and *precious* at the same time.

So if you ever earn more than you need — eat well, rest well, travel far...

And give back. Feed someone. Heal someone. Surprise someone.

Satisfy your mind, body, and soul however you please.

Anyway, back to the hustle:

I used to come home and whine like it was a hostage situation.

"Natasha is driving me crazy."

"This job is trash."

But then I realised — Natasha doesn't pay me.

So she doesn't get to ruin my mood.

Also, my mom's allergic to my dark jokes.

If I ever say, "Ugh, I'll probably die broke," she shoots me a look and goes, "Don't. Saraswati might be sitting on your tongue."

And yeah, it sounds dramatic — but *what if she's right?*

If the universe is listening, I'd rather not manifest struggle.

Because here's what I know for sure:

Money gives you choices. Dignity. Security. Healthcare. A home.

It gets you to the hospital when your throat hurts — and pays for the dan dan noodles you'll eat after.

Money doesn't buy happiness.

But it buys *ease*. And sometimes, that's all happiness needs.

If you have money, your problems might still exist — but they're *sortable*.

If you don't?

Your only problem *will* be money.

So yeah, maybe money can't buy happiness — but have you ever tried being sad in business class?

# CHAPTER SEVENTEEN

# "DON'T WASTE YOUR MONEY ON THINGS"

27 years.

7 travels.

No, I'm not exaggerating.

Grateful for every single one of those trips, but let's be honest — it could have been way more.

My dad doesn't have a single travel gene in his body. My mom? Financially dependent, her Burj Khalifa selfies and Eiffel Tower dreams remained just that — dreams. I guess some cravings are genetic.

So, naturally, childhood was mostly home-based, except for the occasional monitored school trips that felt more like prison breaks with uniforms.

When I grew up, I stopped asking.

Because hearing "no" too many times makes you stop asking altogether.

It becomes easier to just not expect.

But life, as it turns out, has weird ways of giving you what you manifest.

Somehow, I landed a job that literally flies me places — for free.

Irony: Still didn't travel enough.

So one day, I decided to be audacious. I asked my dad.

At age 26.

"Can I go to Kuala Lumpur? My friend's coming from Singapore."

His reply?

"Yes. Send me the details."

I stared at that text like my phone was hacked by aliens.

Was I being catfished by my own father?

Apparently not.

I sent him all the details, exchanged currency with my brother's help, packed my bags, and flew off.

The first moment I stepped into that new country, it still didn't feel real.

Driving through Cameron Highlands.

Eating strawberries with fresh cream on a farm.

Clicking pictures at Hobbiton like a total tourist cliché.

Lounging in massive luxury hotel pools as if I owned the place.

It wasn't just a trip.

It was *the* fuel I never knew I needed to survive the silent mess of adulting.

That pizza — tasteless AF — tasted like a gourmet meal just because I was grateful to afford it.

Mom's handmade laddoos became survival tools more powerful than any emergency contact number.

Those 4 days are now locked safe in my memory forever.

This, my friends, is the *real* effect of money:

It gives you the freedom to make your own choices.

To buy a Barbie merch collection because you never had one as a kid.

To buy a cycle that you ride twice a year but still call *yours*.

To splurge on that random gadget, that useless-but-happy trinket, or that solo trip that nobody understands.

Some of it won't last forever.

Some of it might be totally useless.

But none of it will ever feel like regret.

And please — don't buy your happiness on EMI.

Invest in what makes *you* smile.

Because that's where real wealth begins.

# CHAPTER EIGHTEEN

# "THE TWO MOST IMPORTANT LESSONS IN LIFE"

Love and death — the two scariest teachers you'll ever meet. And nobody prepares you for either.
Sometimes you're a kid in a frock at your grandfather's funeral, not even understanding what's going on. Sometimes you're old enough to know, dressed in dull clothes, wondering how your heart is supposed to cope with this kind of silence.
Nobody teaches us how to deal with loss. I get why. It's uncomfortable, gloomy, something you don't want destiny to bring up at the dinner table. One day someone lives with you, fills your life with memories, and then — they're gone. Just like that.

I was five or six when I lost my grandfather. I don't even remember the rituals, only the way the news was broken to me. I was in the zazziest red skirt and yellow top, ready for a party. My mom quickly changed my clothes, her face wet with tears. That memory still makes me squirm — not because of him, but because of her grief. Funny thing is, the only moment I clearly remember with him isn't grand or profound. I had complained to him that my dadi wouldn't give me ten bucks for a balloon. He looked at her and said, *"Bimla, why aren't you giving her what she's asking?"* That day, I felt like the most powerful kid alive. That's how gentle he was. That's the snapshot I carry.

Then came my nani. My favorite. My safe place.

I woke up one morning to find everyone gone, and my aunt silently dressed me, took me to her house. I thought I'd get my morning hug, but instead I found her lying there, wrapped in white. And my mom—broken in a way I'd never seen before. That image has burned itself into my memory, and I still pray never to see her like that again.

I miss my nani the most. I wanted her to meet my first boyfriend, to gift her a saree from my first salary, to take her on the vacation she always dreamed of. She had less money, but lived the richest life — something I'm still trying to learn from her every single day.

In the last few years, I've lost the rest of my

grandparents too. Each loss felt different. And honestly, I don't want to talk more about it — because no one really wants to feel sad again, do they?

Here's the thing about death: it's inevitable, sure. But the part no one tells you is this — you end up living by them. You inherit their habits, their quirks, their silly sayings. You start using their old mugs, their favourite expressions. Time doesn't erase them. It reshapes them. People say time heals, but I think time teaches. It teaches you to be grateful for the life you have, to love harder, to be kinder, to loosen your grip on all the things that don't matter. And maybe to be a little less afraid of the end. But the void they leave? That's the real challenge. No more nagging smiles, no more "when are you getting married" conversations, no more earthy presence filling the room. Just echoes.

I've lost both pairs now. And I'm still learning how to cope. But I know one thing: it does get lighter. God has a way of placing people in your life to soften the sharp edges of grief. And if not, maybe it just means He already made you strong enough to hold it yourself. Tiny note here: when you're hurting, it's so easy to look up at the ceiling and ask, *"Why me?"* But I've come to believe God has a kind of pain meter. He dials it to exactly what He knows you can survive. Not an ounce more, not an ounce less. It sounds philosophical, I know. But I learned it the hard way.

And maybe that's the point. Lesson one and lesson two — love and death — they can't be taught. They can only be felt and lived.

If this is the last page you're reading today, let it feel less like a goodbye and more like the kind of hug that lingers — the kind where no one rushes to pull away.

Just one thing to remember: life is too short to not know its worth.

And sometimes, knowing its worth is as simple as pausing long enough to feel the quiet joy in your own heartbeat. Hold that. Protect that.

So when you put this book away, look around — life already has the jalebi for your sweet tooth, the kaadha for your cough, and a joke for everything else. All it needs is for you to join in.

* 9 7 8 1 8 0 7 1 5 3 3 9 7 *